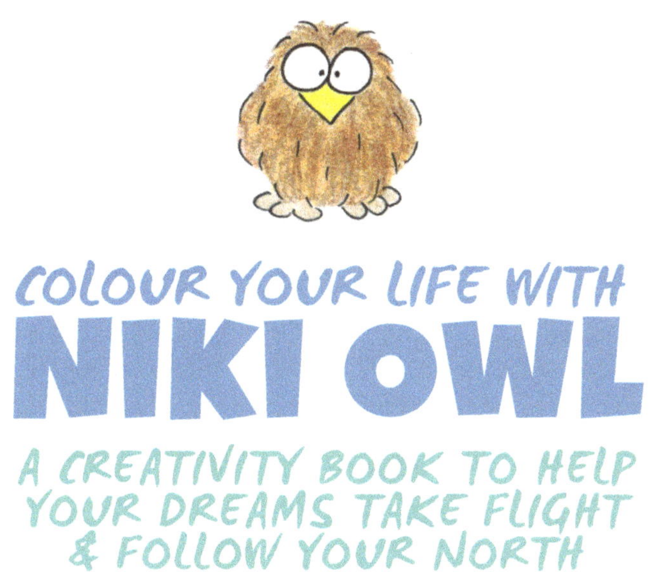

COLOUR YOUR LIFE WITH
NIKI OWL

A CREATIVITY BOOK TO HELP YOUR DREAMS TAKE FLIGHT & FOLLOW YOUR NORTH

WRITTEN & ILLUSTRATED BY
KARIN PINTER

Published by Niki Owl Books.

Colour Your Life with Niki Owl - A Creativity Book to Help Your Dreams Take Flight & Follow Your North.
Copyright © 2018 by Karin Pinter.

ISBN 978-0-9964416-1-2
Words, Illustrations and Design by Karin Pinter.

Printed on acid-free paper at a geographical region closest to you.

Visit NikiOwl.com

FOR THE KID IN YOU, WHO UNDERSTANDS THAT LIFE IS A BIG ADVENTURE

And for Dad, the first person who
inspired me to live Big Adventures
and go explore the world.

everything is imagined first, and then it is created...

All great explorers and inventors took a leap of faith on their vision. They didn't really know what would happen as they embarked on new adventures or creations, although they did it anyway, and it's through their courage and inspiration that many discoveries were made.

We take leaps of faith every day simply stepping out into the world and following what's in our hearts. Although without nourishing the very things that light us up, we can get lost in the busy-ness of life, forgetting to use our creativity and imagination. As a result, we stop creating with life and simply react to it. Life can become stagnant, as cherished dreams become distant visions that feel out of reach. This is true whether you're a teenager or you're well into your career and family life.

This book is designed to help you focus your imagination on things that light you up, and integrate them into your day-to-day. It's a gateway to your imagination and a creative space to birth the dreams in your heart that are ready to leap into this world, because every dream matters, including yours!

Your inner kid knows exactly what those dreams are, because he or she is always in there whispering ideas and guidance for you to play and co-create with life.

You'll be accompanied on this journey by our adventurous co-pilot in creation, Niki Owl, who will support and encourage your inner wisdom to unfold.

Maybe you haven't drawn or used colouring pencils in ages, or you feel like you "can't draw". Do no let that hold you back. Simply let your imagination and inner guidance surprise you. Life is about allowing beautiful surprises to happen!

Listen to the joyful whispers,
Karin

HOW TO USE THIS BOOK...

Your best experience of this book will be to use colouring pencils and your favorite pen or pencil to write with.

The pages are laid out to build on the core themes, so I suggest you fill in the Dreams pages (4 & 5) first and carry on from there. Go at the pace of your inspiration!

As your thoughts and clarity begin to flow, you may find yourself going back to previous pages and adding to what you wrote or drew earlier.

Fill in any blank spaces with things that come up as you go through the book. This is your personal creative space, so make of it as you please!

JUST SO YOU KNOW...

The illustrations in this book are from a very special place in Canada where I took one of my biggest leaps of faith and where the first Niki Owl novel was "born" - Vancouver, BC. At the end of the book you'll find a list of the different landmarks.

BEFORE YOU BEGIN, MEET YOUR CO-PILOT...
NIKI OWL

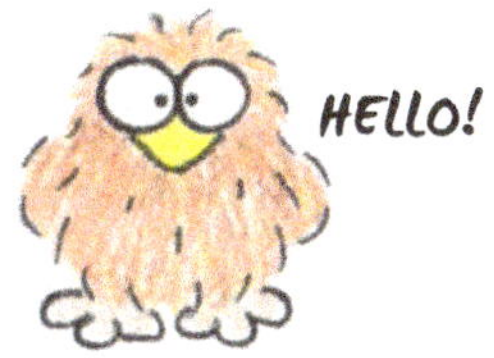

NIKI LOVES TO TRAVEL, EXPLORE DIFFERENT CULTURES, TAKE CARE OF NATURE AND HIS FELLOW BEINGS, EAT COOKIES, AND PUT A SMILE IN PEOPLE'S HEARTS. HE ALSO LOVES HUGS & SUNSHINE (ALTHOUGH A COZY FIREPLACE ON A RAINY DAY IS WONDERFUL TOO). AND HE THINKS YOU'RE REALLY COOL.

I'd love to see what you create! If you're inspired to share, take some photos and post them online (social media handles at the end of the book). You can also send an email to hello@NikiOwl.com with your comments on what this book is helping you create in your life.

THERE ARE DREAMS THAT LIVE IN OUR HEARTS, AND **DREAMS THAT COME TO LIFE...**

THE DIFFERENCE BETWEEN THEM IS
A LEAP OF FAITH
(AND ACTIONS TO MAKE THEM HAPPEN!)

ARE YOU READY TO CREATE YOUR DREAMS?

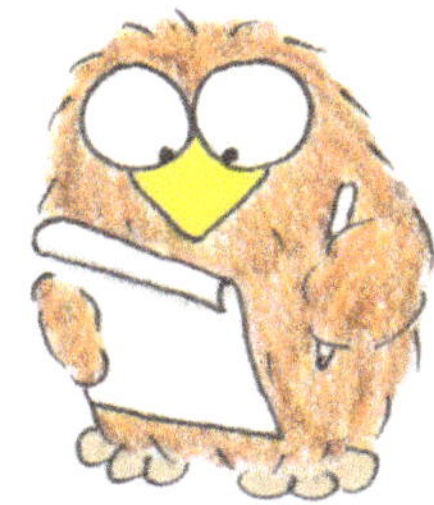

DECLARATION OF CREATIVITY & IMAGINATION

I GIVE MYSELF PERMISSION TO TAKE A LEAP OF FAITH ON MY DREAMS BY NOURISHING MY IMAGINATION, EXPLORING MY CREATIVITY & FOLLOWING MY TRUE NORTH!

SIGNED: _______________________________

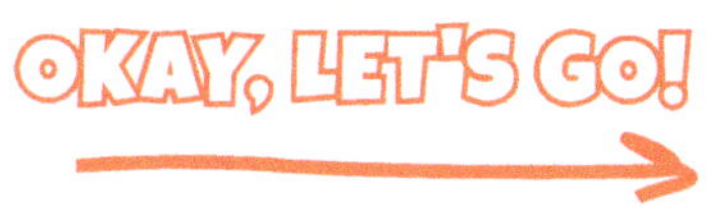

A FUN FACT FOR THE EXPLORER IN YOU...

On the cover of this book, Niki is standing on a rock structure called an Inukshuk. This kind of monument is made out of unworked stones and is used by the Inuit* for communication or as markers to define a path, among other things.

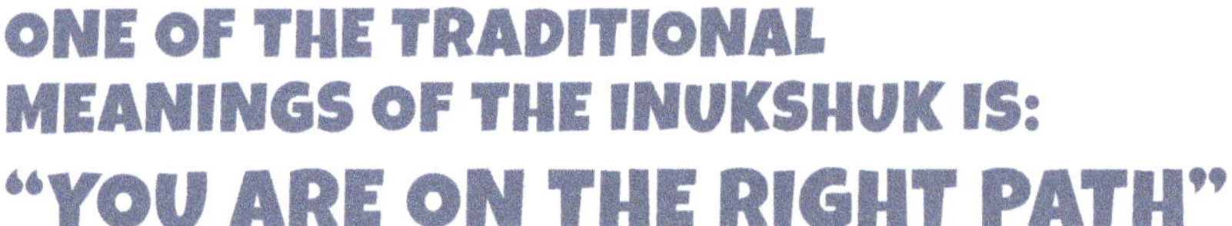

ONE OF THE TRADITIONAL MEANINGS OF THE INUKSHUK IS:
"YOU ARE ON THE RIGHT PATH"

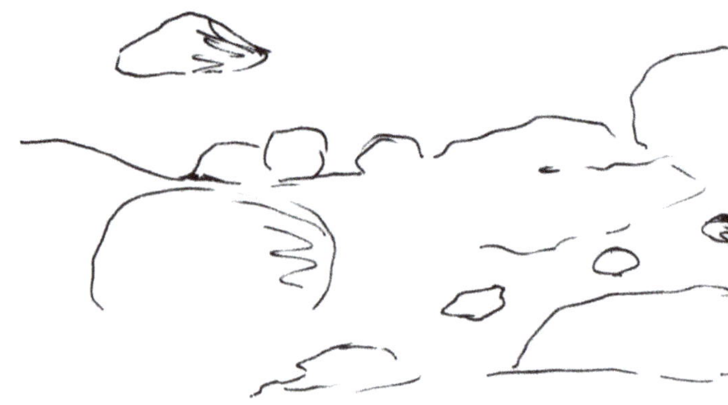

LET'S EXPLORE WHAT THAT IS FOR YOU AND YOUR DREAMS...

* The Inuit are indigenous peoples of similar cultures who inhabit the Arctic regions of Canada, Greenland, Siberia & Alaska. They have a rich connection with nature.

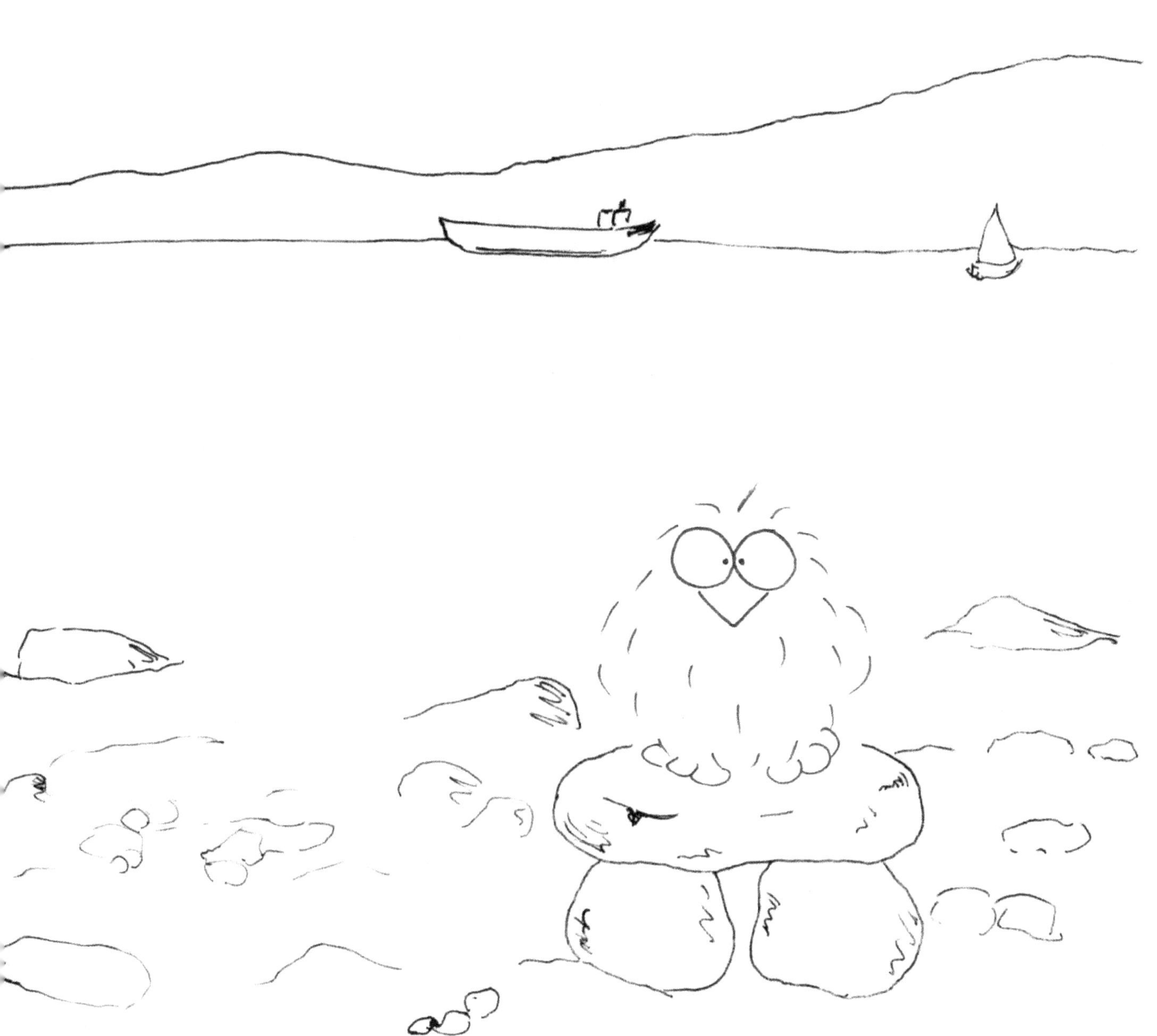

WE'LL START WITH YOUR DREAMS

WHAT KEEPS YOU CURIOUS ABOUT GETTING UP EVERY DAY TO EXPLORE THIS BEAUTIFUL WORLD?

WRITE YOUR DREAMS HERE!

↓

THINK OF THINGS YOU'D LOVE TO EXPERIENCE, CREATE, PLACES TO VISIT, IDEAS YOU HAVE...

AWESOME! NOW LET'S TALK ABOUT LOVE... WHAT MAKES YOU LOVE YOUR LIFE?

Think of experiences, places, people and relationships you value, things that add quality to your life and make you feel good.

WRITE & DRAW THEM HERE!

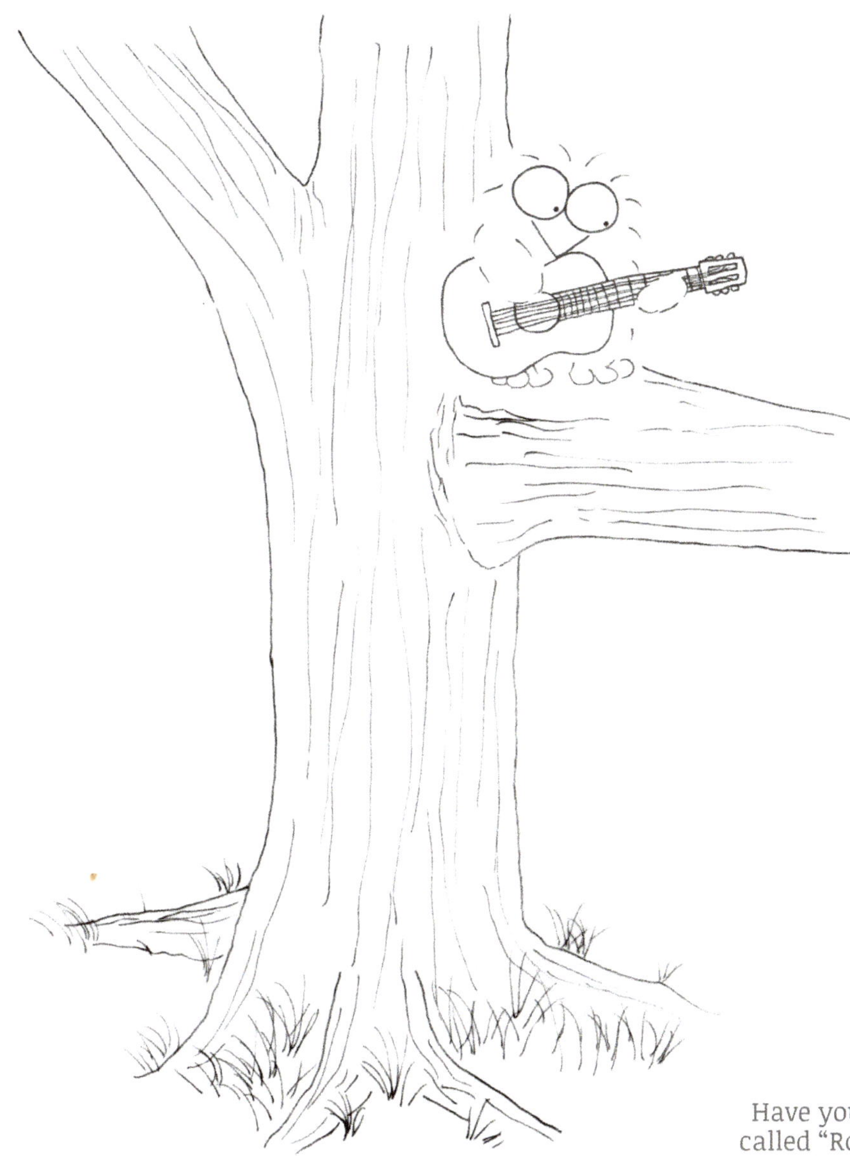

Have you ever heard a tune
called "Romance Anónimo"?
Niki is playing it on his guitar.

NEXT UP IS
JOY... ALSO KNOWN AS YOUR "HAPPY PLACE"

WHAT LIGHTS YOU UP?

It's easy to get caught up making others happy, but what about making time for YOUR personal joy? You know, investing time and energy in activities you do by yourself that tune you into your personal essence? For example, singing, writing, drawing, painting, playing an instrument, kicking a ball, going for walks, being at a lake or a beach...

WRITE & DRAW THEM HERE!

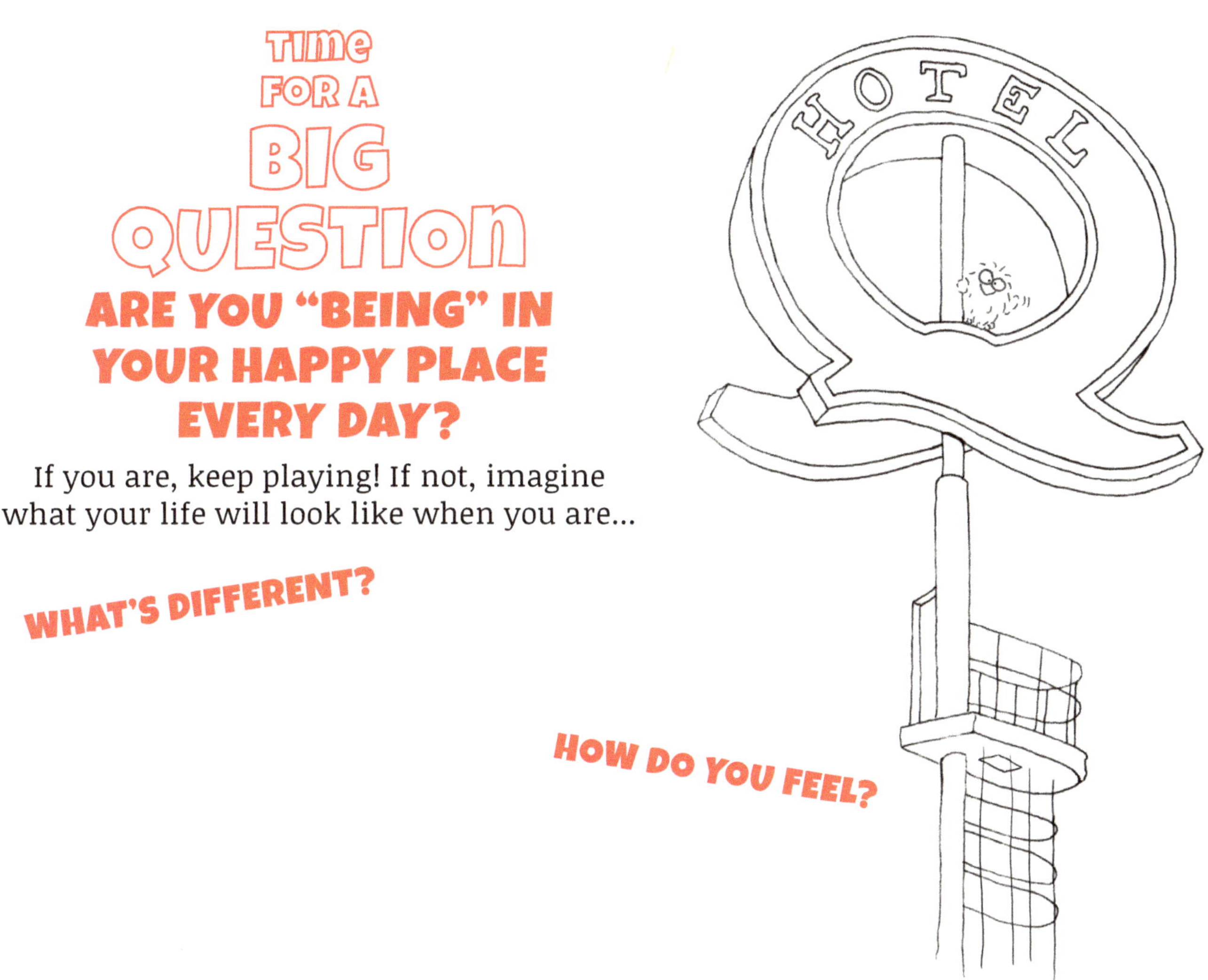

TIME FOR A BIG QUESTION

ARE YOU "BEING" IN YOUR HAPPY PLACE EVERY DAY?

If you are, keep playing! If not, imagine what your life will look like when you are...

WHAT'S DIFFERENT?

HOW DO YOU FEEL?

HOW ARE YOU LIVING?

NOW IMAGINE...

YOUR WORLD FILLED WITH POSSIBILITIES READY TO BE DISCOVERED

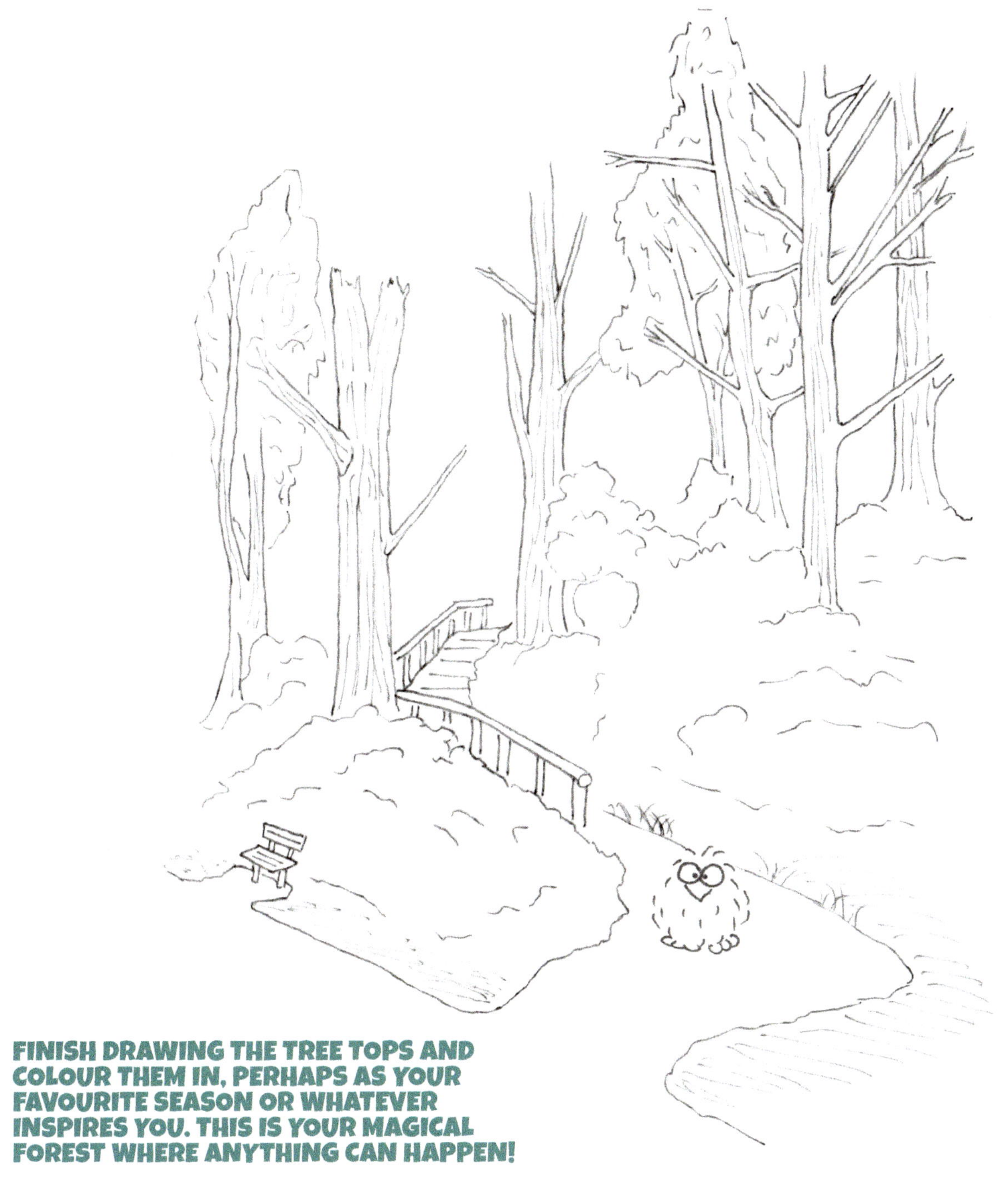

FINISH DRAWING THE TREE TOPS AND COLOUR THEM IN, PERHAPS AS YOUR FAVOURITE SEASON OR WHATEVER INSPIRES YOU. THIS IS YOUR MAGICAL FOREST WHERE ANYTHING CAN HAPPEN!

WHERE YOU BOLDLY CROSS THE BRIDGE AND THE UNKNOWN BECOMES KNOWN...

WHERE ADVENTURE IS ONE LEAP OF WONDER AFTER ANOTHER!

The next page might seem like a simple drawing of a bridge in the middle of a forest, although for many people, crossing a bridge can symbolise overcoming their fears.

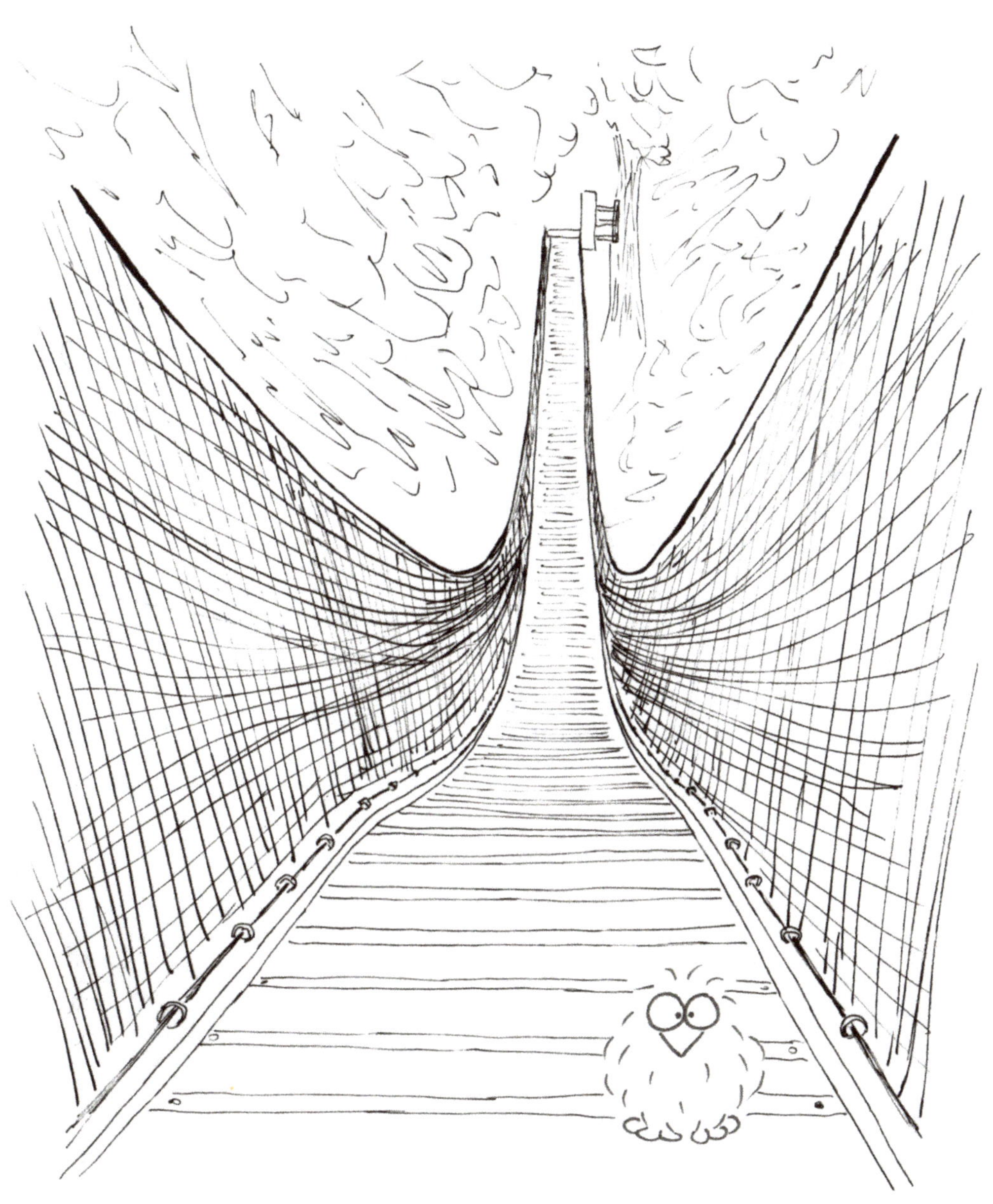

THIS KIND OF

CURIOSITY

LEADS TO

CREATION

AND HELPS YOU

MARVEL

AT HOW OUR

UNIVERSE

TICKS...

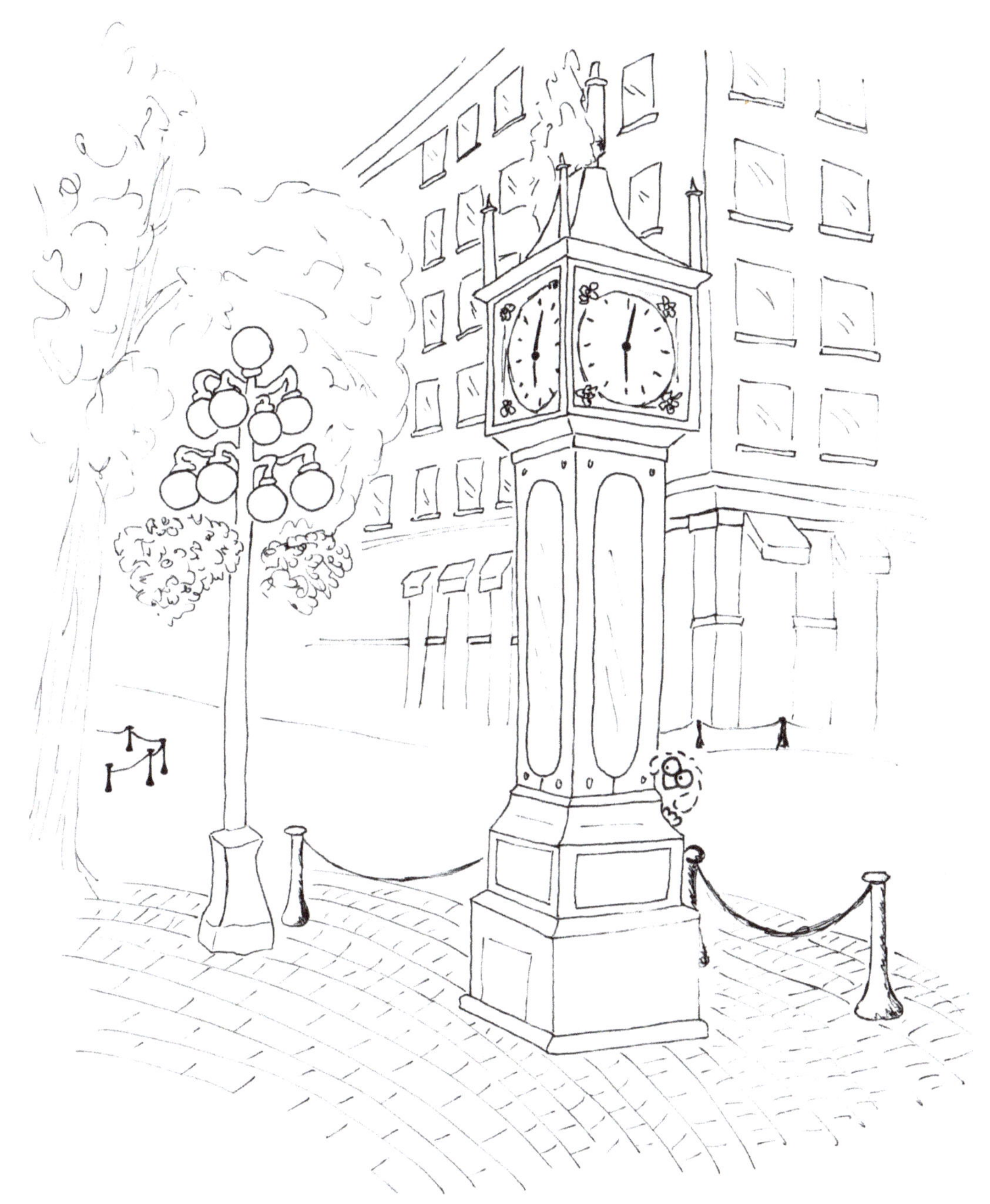

OH, AND JUST IN CASE YOU WERE WONDERING...
(BECAUSE IT CAN FEEL LONELY OUT THERE AT TIMES)

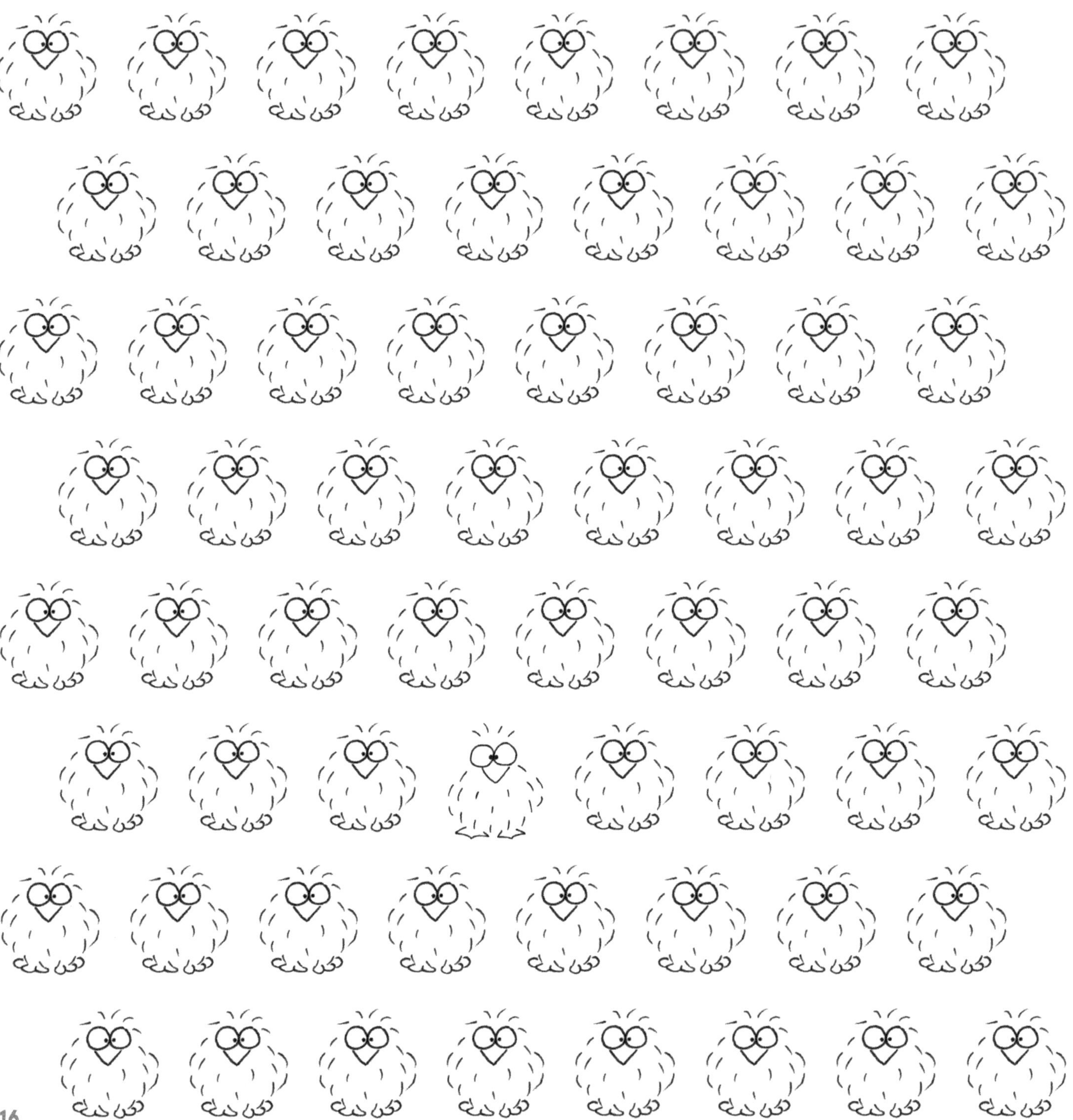

YOU BELONG HERE WITH OWL OF US

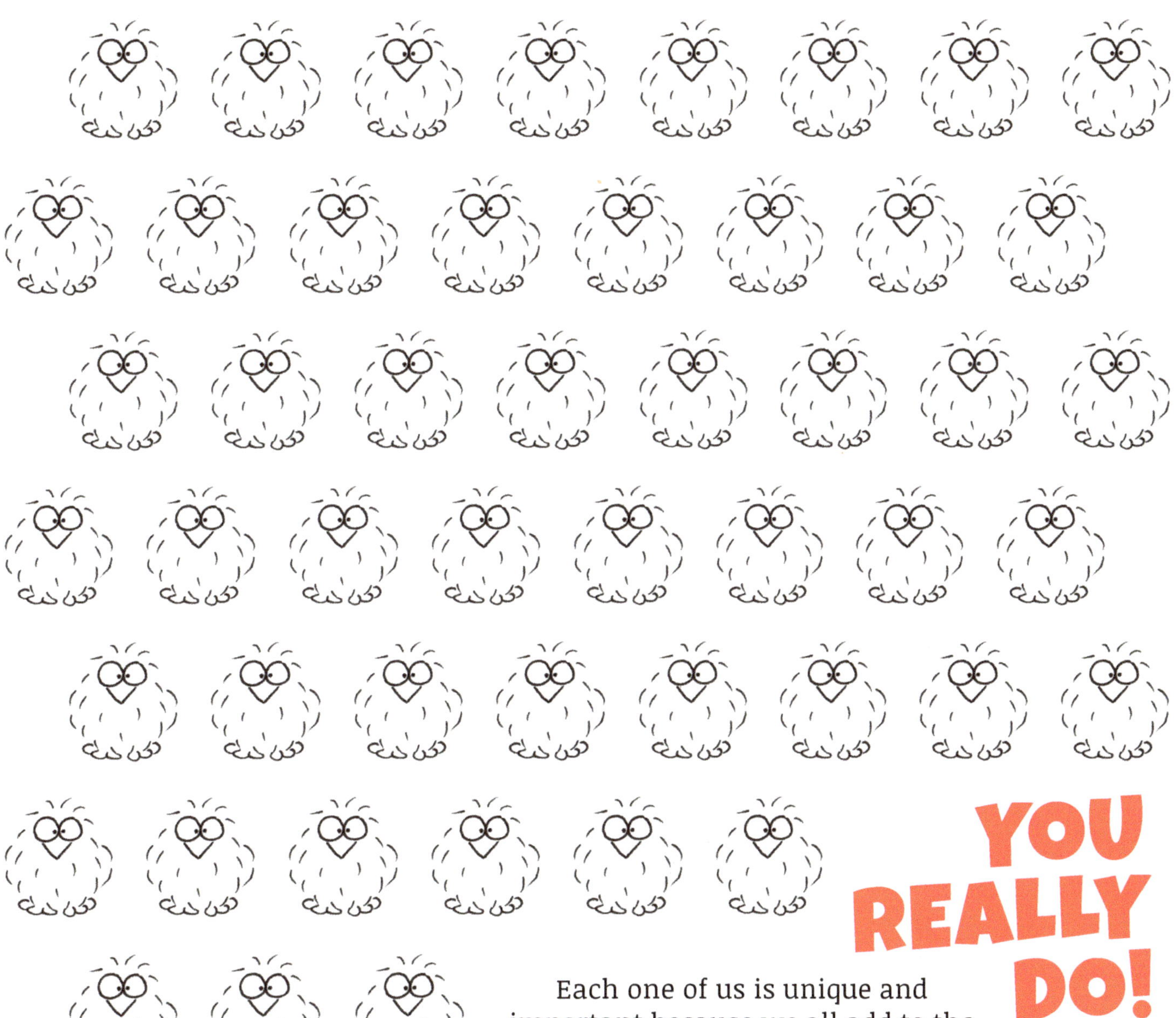

YOU
REALLY
DO!

Each one of us is unique and important because we all add to the beautiful diversity of life...

ATTITUDE DETERMINES OWLTITUDE

LET YOUR IMAGINATION FLY HIGH

REFLECTION: DOES YOUR ATTITUDE NEED AN UPGRADE?

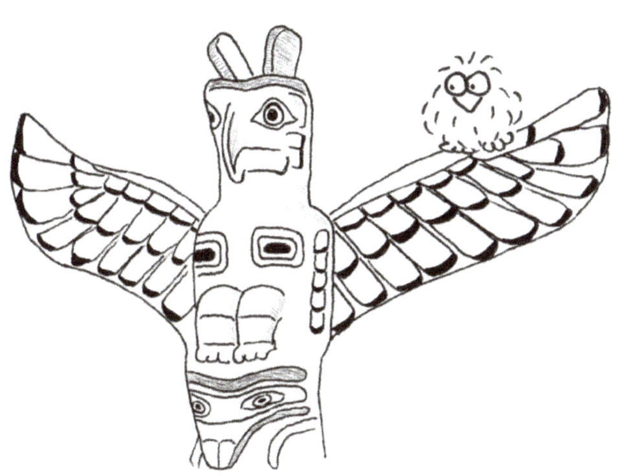

A TOTEM POLE USUALLY REPRESENTS SPECIAL FORCES AND ATTRIBUTES. WHILST IT IS USUALLY MADE UP OF IMAGES OF BIRDS AND ANIMALS, YOU CAN COMPLETE YOURS BY DRAWING AND WRITING THINGS THAT ARE MEANINGFUL TO YOU AND THAT ELEVATE YOUR SPIRIT.

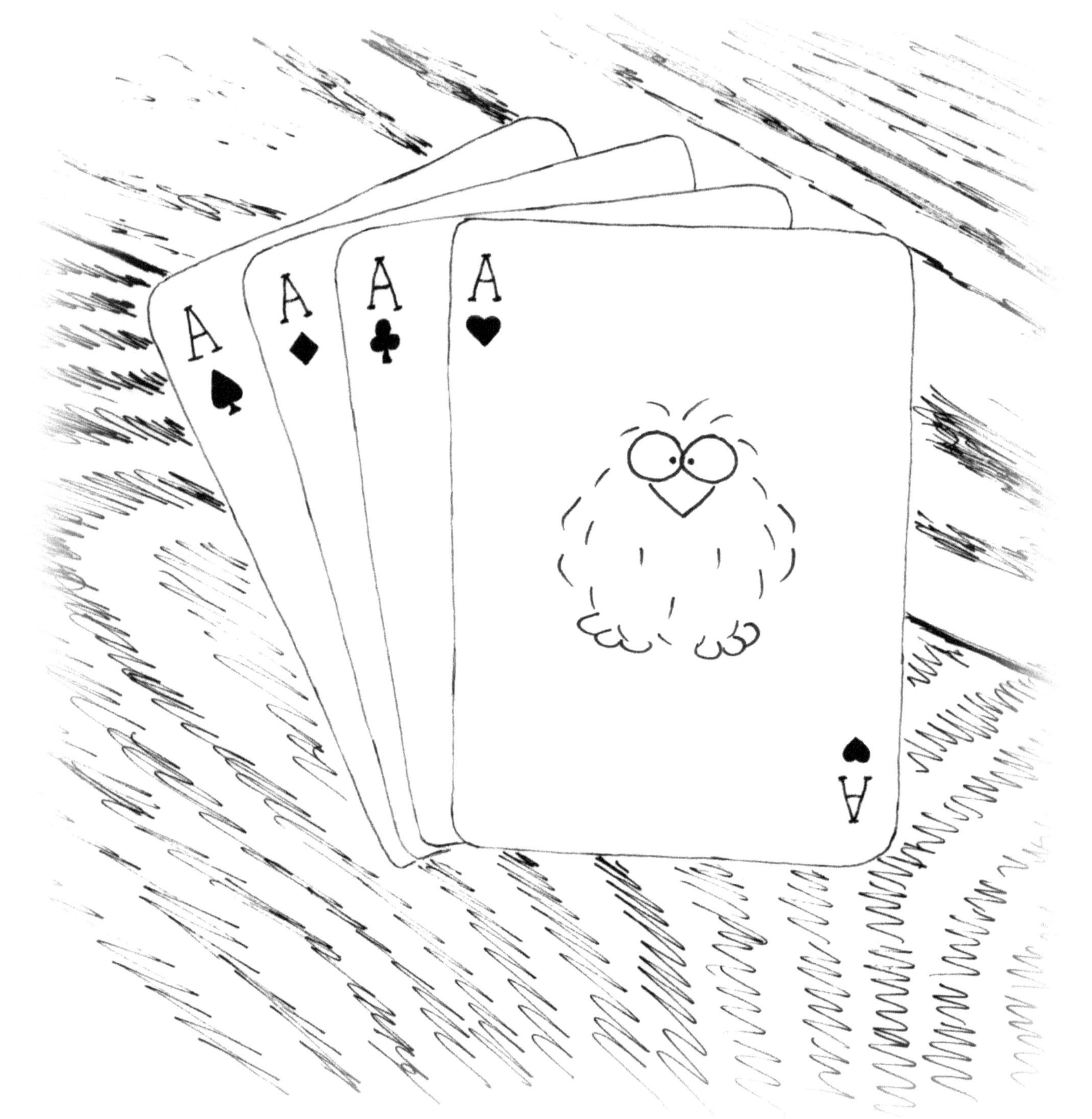

A
A
A
A

NOW THAT YOU'RE FOCUSED ON FEELING GOOD,
IT'S IMPORTANT TO REMEMBER...

FEELING GOOD LEADS TO CLARITY
CLARITY LEADS TO DECISION
DECISION DRIVES ACTION

BUT WHERE THE **REAL MAGIC** HAPPENS
IS IN THE BELIEF, BECAUSE...

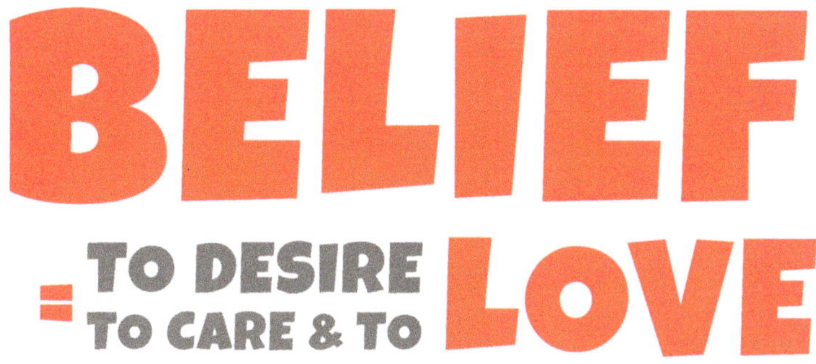

THIS IS THE **ACE** EACH ONE OF US
CARRIES IN OUR **HEARTS** BECAUSE...

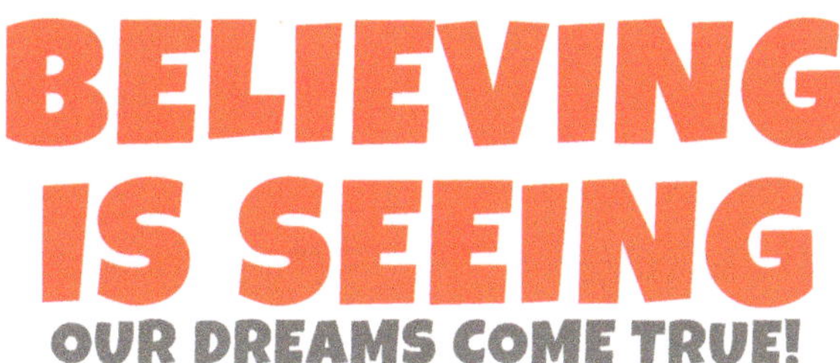

OUR DREAMS COME TRUE!

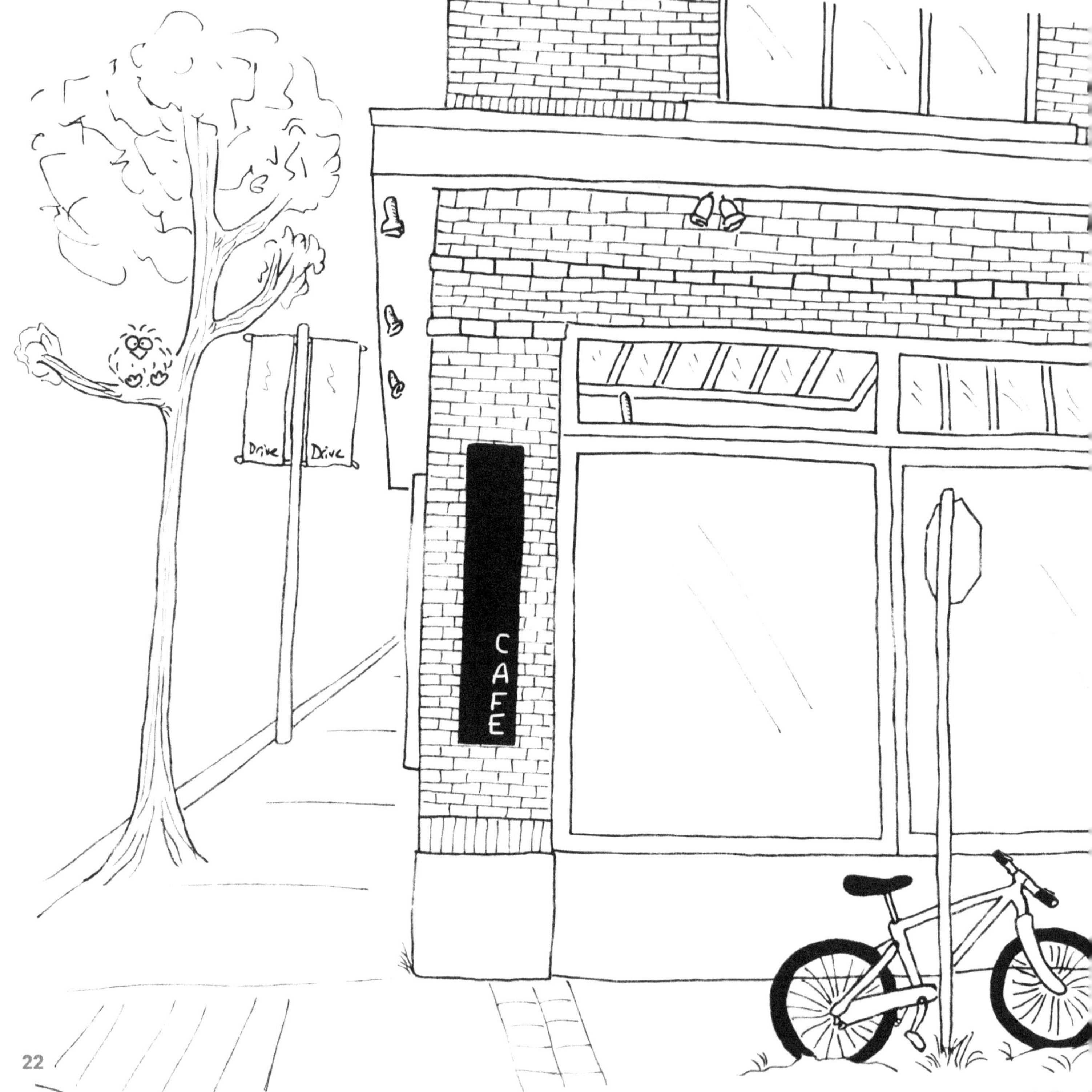

Drive
Drive
CAFE

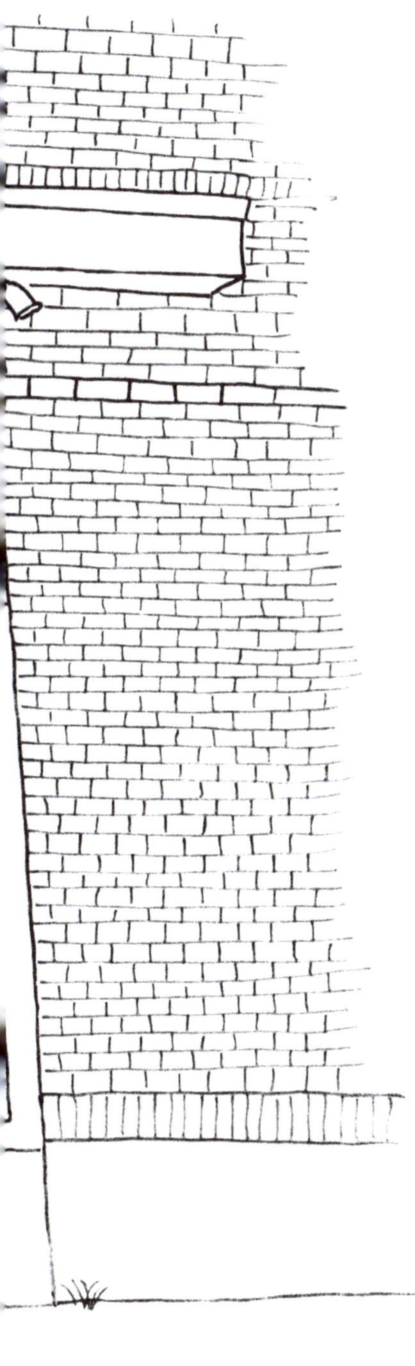
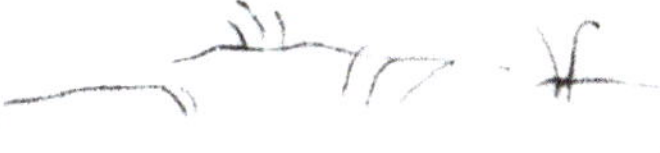

LIFE IS A CONSTANT CYCLE OF AWARENESS TO ACTUALIZE YOUR DREAMS

KEEP LISTENING TO YOUR HEART AND FOLLOW THE SIGNS WHEN THEY SHOW UP

WHEN YOU'RE NOT SURE WHICH DIRECTION TO TAKE...

GO IN THE DIRECTION OF WHAT MAKES YOU FEEL ALIVE AND TICKLES YOUR INSPIRATION!

IT'S A GOOD WAY TO LIVE EVERY DAY

OUR PUREST PURPOSE IS TO LOVE... SO WHEN YOU MATCH WHAT LOVE WITH WHAT YOU DO YOU'RE LIVING A PURPOSEFUL LIFE!

Purpose comes from how we feel we can best help our fellow human beings with our many gifts, skills, talents and energy. These are what guide us toward our True North, and the things we can "do" to live it. What activities make you feel like you're living purposefully?

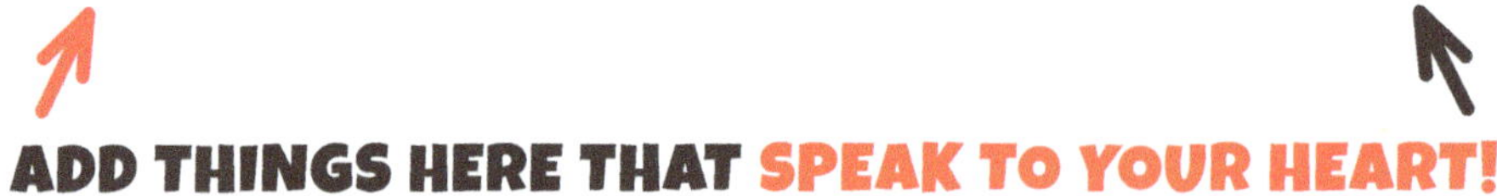

NOW LET'S GET YOUR INNER COMPASS CALIBRATED
WITH THE 4 ELEMENTS THAT KEEP YOU ON COURSE...

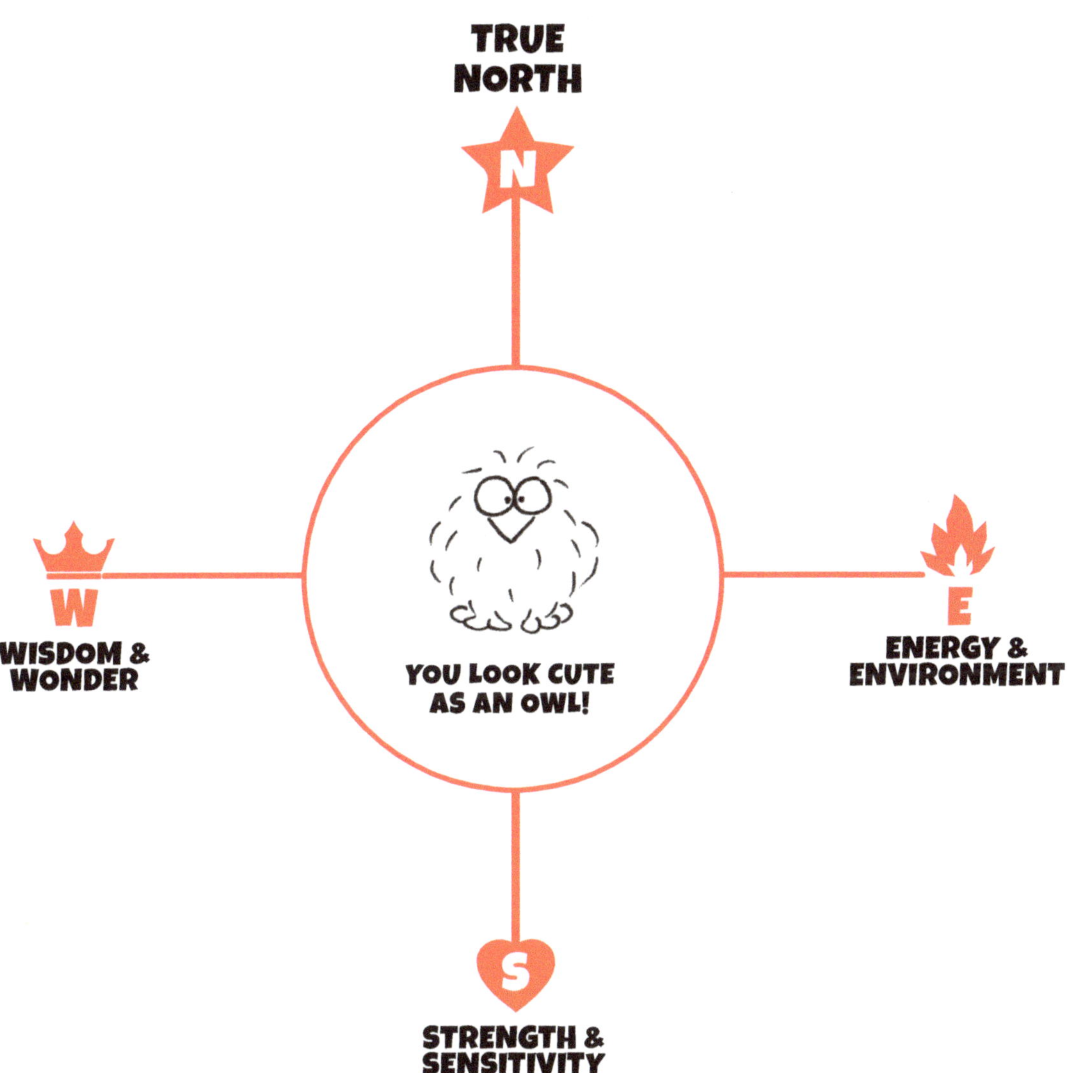

TRUE
NORTH
N
WISDOM &
WONDER
W
YOU LOOK CUTE
AS AN OWL!
E
ENERGY &
ENVIRONMENT
S
STRENGTH &
SENSITIVITY

WE'LL EXPLORE THEM IN THE NEXT PAGES!

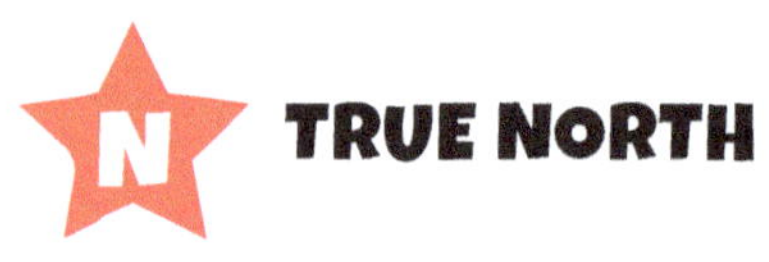 **TRUE NORTH**

Just as a clear night is key to see the stars and navigate the ocean, inner clarity is key to seeing the signs line up along your path and follow your True North. Let's reflect on this for a moment...

WHAT DO YOU FEEL DRAWN TOWARDS?

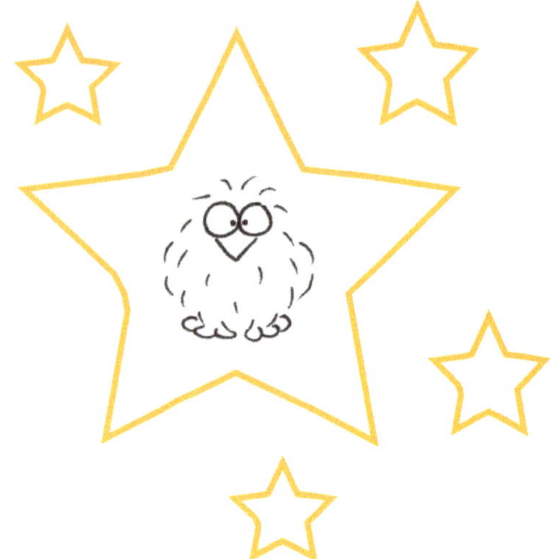

ARE YOU MOVING IN THAT DIRECTION?

IF NOT, WHAT IS IN THE WAY & HOW CAN YOU CLEAR YOUR PATH?

LOOKS LIKE NIKI OWL NEEDS SOMETHING TO PERCH ON
WHILE YOU EXPLORE YOUR TRUE NORTH. WILL YOU DRAW IT?
IT MAY JUST GIVE YOU INSIGHTS ON YOUR DIRECTION!

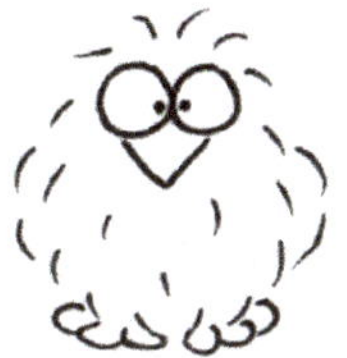

EXPLORER'S TIP!
WHEN MOVING TOWARDS YOUR TRUE NORTH,
ASK FOR REALLY CLEAR SIGNS TO REVEAL THEMSELVES,
AND BE OPEN TO ACTING ON THEM AS THEY SHOW UP...

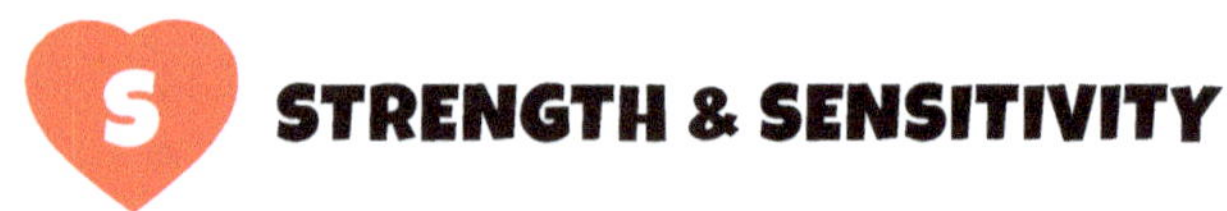

STRENGTH & SENSITIVITY

SOME PEOPLE THINK SENSITIVITY IS A WEAKNESS. NOT TRUE!

YOUR SENSITIVITY IS AN EXCEPTIONAL QUALITY THAT MAKES YOU WHO YOU ARE AND NOURISHES YOUR INNER STRENGTH.

THIS COMBINATION HELPS YOU FACE ANY CHALLENGE AND DREAM, AND CREATE GREAT THINGS WITH HUMILITY AND HEALTHY PRIDE.

WHAT ARE YOUR STRENGTHS & SENSITIVITIES?
(THINK OF HIDDEN TREASURES WITHIN YOU)

You can also ask your friends, family and colleagues what they see in you!

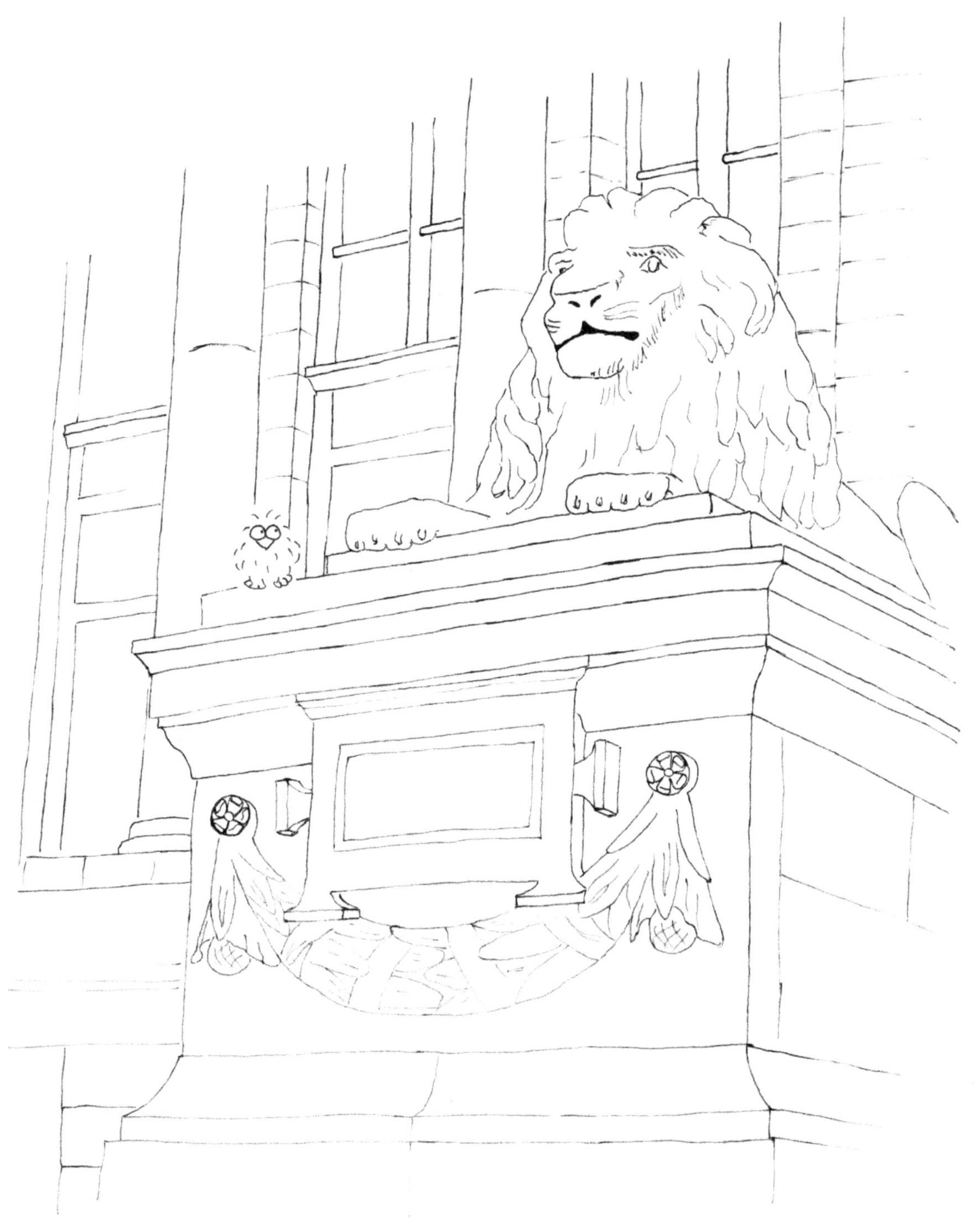

YOUR HEART IS FILLED WITH WISDOM
JUST LISTEN TO THE WHISPERS... WHAT ARE THEY TELLING YOU?

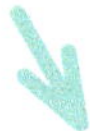

WHEN YOU LIVE IN WONDER & APPRECIATE THE BEAUTY WITHIN YOU
LIFE SHOWERS YOU WITH PLENTY OF GOOD STUFF LIKE LEAVES SWIRLING AROUND ON A BREEZY DAY...

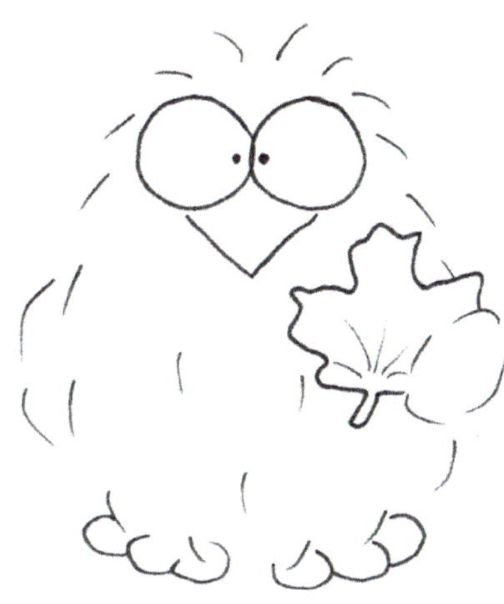

SPEAKING OF LEAVES,
WE COULD USE SOME MORE HERE PLEASE
(ADD ANYTHING ELSE YOU LIKE)

WHAT ARE YOUR DREAM ENERGY EFFICIENCY & ENVIRONMENT LIKE?

Living your True North and creating dreams is like mastering an instrument - they require daily attention and action to make progress. This also means ensuring you have energy for your dreams, not just the basic day-to-day activities of life.

Do you eat well, sleep well, do you dedicate time for dreams and creativity? What little shifts can you make in your daily activities to create space for your dreams to progress? Are your surroundings conducive to your flow of creative energy?

A SPECIAL NOTE ON HOW THE WAY WE MANAGE OUR ENERGY & TIME IMPACTS OUR DREAMS COMING TO LIFE...

It's easy to let the busy-ness of life "take over" how we manage our time, but the concept of time is simply a way to manage our energy, so we actually get to make time work for us!

Do you put your dreams and ideas off into some unspecified time in the future by telling yourself, "Some day I'll do that..."? Let's change that now!

WRITE SOME DREAMS BELOW AND PUT A DATE NEXT TO THEM (AS IT JUMPS INTO YOUR MIND). SEE WHAT HAPPENS!

THIS BRINGS US BACK TO
USING YOUR IMAGINATION
TO GIVE LIFE TO YOUR DREAMS & ASPIRATIONS

Now that you're navigating towards your True North, let's look at your next steps. Creating a Dream Map is a great way to start!

1. ACTIVATE YOUR SENSES AND IMAGINATION

You're going to begin with the end in mind. Meaning, think of your dream (the North Star on the map) as if it has already come true. Immerse yourself in the experience:
How do you feel achieving it? What do you see? What do you hear?

2. DISCOVER YOUR NEXT STEPS

Now, start thinking backwards as you let your mind reveal the key actions and steps that you took along the way that will bring you back to the present moment. Write and/or draw these on your map, as they show up. Let your intuition guide you.

Example: if you want to publish a book, think of it as though it's already been published ("My Dream" on the map). Before this you will have sent your manuscript to your editor for review. Before this you will have completed the manuscript. Before this you will have thought about what type of book you'd like to write. And before this, your heart will have lit up with the inspiration to write a book ("Where I am now" on the map). See how your mind has guided you backward, to now? Now you have a plan of action. By taking the first step forward, you'll discover other details along the way, though at least you have a starting point and basic route to follow and complete.

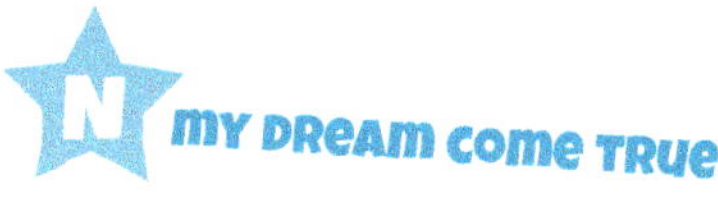

YOUR DREAMS MATTER!

WHERE I AM NOW 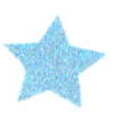

AWESOME!

Small steps are usually easier to integrate into your daily life. They will help you make progress without going into overwhelm and putting things off (which is where many people get stuck on their dreams!).

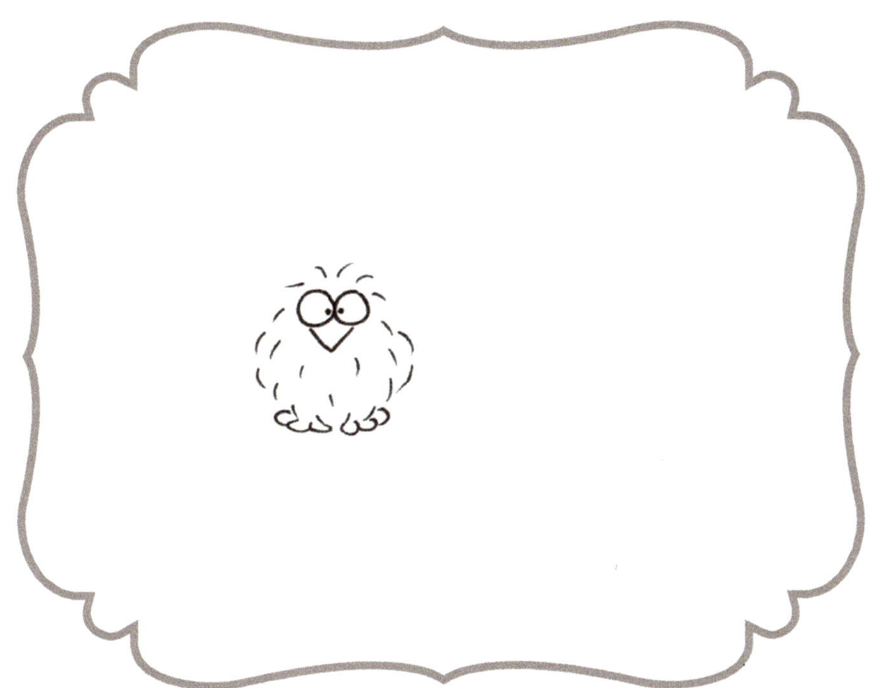

DRAW YOUR CARTOON SELF NEXT TO NIKI

If you ever find yourself exploring the beautiful city of Vancouver, here's a list of the places and momuments you've just seen in the book:

Jericho Beach   p. 2-3
Lonsdale Quay, North Shore   p. 9
English Bay/Stanley Park   p. 11
Lynn Canyon bridge, North Vancouver   p. 13
Gastown Steam Clock   p. 15
Kakaso'Las Totem Pole at Brockton Point, Stanley Park   p. 19
Coffee shop at East 4th & Commercial Drive   p. 22-23
Vancouver Art Gallery   p. 29

Have fun!!!

And if you happen to this book with you, why not take a picture of yourself with it at any one of these landmarks? You can tag Niki Owl on any of his social networks (see next page).

DID YOU ENJOY THIS BOOK?

Discover more books, colouring pages, gifts and other
fun stuff on NikiOwl.com

HANG OUT WITH NIKI OWL

Facebook.com/NikiOwl
Instagram: @NikiOwl
Twitter: @NikiOwl

SEND LOVE NOTES

Hello@NikiOwl.com (yes, owls can write emails too!)

ABOUT KARIN PINTER

Karin's love for writing, drawing and creativity comes from her early childhood. She created Niki Owl in her teens as a way to channel her imagination and inspire joy in others through her illustrated character.

Karin's first novel "Niki Owl, Leap of Faith" tells the story of Niki Owl as he takes a leap of faith and adjusts to a new life in Canada after leaving his home country. It touches on the universal topics we encounter as we adapt to major life changes and new situations.

This Niki Owl Creativity Book was created as a way to help people get in touch with their inner kid, activate their imagination and bring creativity into their everyday lives so they can take their own leaps of faith at any "age."

CONNECT WITH KARIN

KarinPinter.com
Hello@KarinPinter.com
Facebook.com/KarinPinterOfficial
Twitter: @KarinPinter
Instagram: @Karin.Pinter

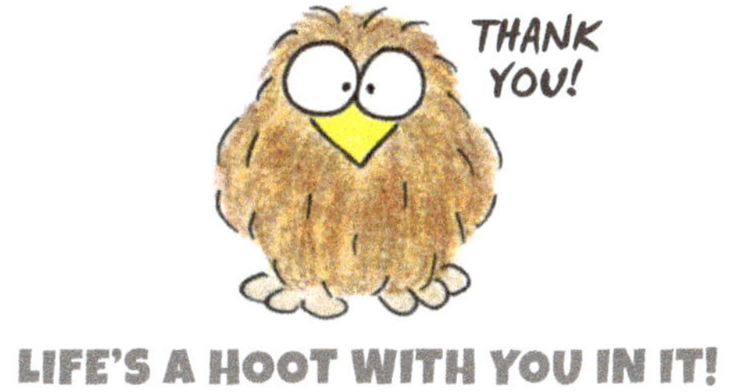

LIFE'S A HOOT WITH YOU IN IT!

www.ingramcontent.com/pod-product-compliance
Lightning Source LLC
Chambersburg PA
CBHW042052030726
47599CB00019B/2462